JENNIFER GALLAGHER

The Gold Ticket

CORNELSEN
ENGLISH
LIBRARY

CORNELSEN **ENGLISH** LIBRARY
Jennifer Gallagher · The Gold Ticket

Verlagsredaktion
Doreen Arnold; Bonnie Glänzer

Umschlaggestaltung
hawemannundmosch, Konzeption und Gestaltung, Berlin

Titelbild
Fotolia/Malgortzata Kistryn (Löwenkopf (M)); Shutterstock/Adrian Hughes
(Ticket (M))

Illustration
M. B. Schulz, Düsseldorf

Gestaltung & technische Umsetzung
Buchgestaltung + Berlin

www.cornelsen.de

1. Auflage, 5. Druck 2025

Alle Drucke dieser Auflage sind inhaltlich unverändert und können
im Unterricht nebeneinander verwendet werden.

Druck: H. Heenemann, Berlin

ISBN 978-3-06-033076-8

PEFC-zertifiziert

Dieses Produkt
stammt aus
nachhaltig
bewirtschafteten
Wäldern

PEFC/04-31-1156   www.pefc.de

CONTENTS

CHAPTER 1

'Justin, breakfast is almost ready!'

Justin slowly opened one eye and then the other. He looked at the clock near his bed.

'Mum's mad,' he thought. 'It's Saturday, it's the school
5 holidays so there's no school, and it's only 10 o'clock.'

He didn't want to get up yet – it was too warm and comfortable. But his mother shouted from the kitchen again.

'Come on, love. I have to leave soon.'

10 'OK, I'm coming,' Justin shouted back. He didn't want his mother to come upstairs and into his room. His clothes, computer stuff and school books were all over the floor, and he didn't want his mother to shout about that!

Ten minutes later, Justin came into the kitchen and sat at
15 the table.

'Where are you going?' Justin asked. 'It's so early.'

His mother smiled at him.

'I have to go to the supermarket,' she said. 'Then I want to visit Grandma. Do you want to come with me?'

20 'Is it OK if I don't come?' said Justin.

'That's fine. Don't forget it's her birthday soon – maybe you can make her a special card or something.'

'Cool, I can do it on the computer.'

'OK, love. See you later. There are some sandwiches
25 and fruit in the fridge for your lunch. Stay out of trouble!'

'Ha, ha, that's very funny. Bye, Mum.'

Justin went upstairs to his room. 'She really is mad,' he thought. 'How can I get into trouble when I just stay here and make a birthday card for the best grandma in the world? There's no way!'

5　　Justin turned on his computer.

'Now, what kind of picture can I put on her card?' he thought. 'She likes birds because she always goes on long walks to watch them through her binoculars. She also likes lions. I have a really cool photo of the lions at the
10　Safari Park so maybe I can …'

Suddenly, Justin's mobile phone beeped. It was a text from Sam:

What r U doing 2day?
Call me when U wake up ;-)
15　**I have an idea.**

'Hmmm, I wonder what his idea is,' thought Justin. He called Sam.

'Hi. You're up early,' said Sam.

'Ha ha. So are you,' laughed Justin. 'What's up?'

20　'There's a jumble sale today near Drake Circus shopping centre.'

'A what?'

'A jumble sale. You know, where you can buy second-hand stuff. Do you want to go with me?'

25　'Hmmm, it sounds boring.'

'Well, there's usually some cool cheap stuff at jumble sales – like old cameras and clocks. You collect things like that, don't you?'

'Yes, that's true but I wanted to make a birthday card
30　for my grandma today.'

'Are you going to give her a present, too? Maybe you can find something nice for her at the jumble sale.'

'OK, you're right,' said Justin. 'I have to text Mum and ask her first, but I'm sure it's OK. What time do you want to meet?'

'At 2 o'clock outside the shopping centre. OK?'

5 'Sure.' said Justin. 'See you then.'

When Justin arrived at the Drake Circus shopping centre, he couldn't see Sam because there were so many people.

'Maybe this isn't a good idea,' he thought. 'Saturdays are always so busy. Why does everyone go shopping on a
10 Saturday?'

Then he heard someone shout his name.

'Justin, I'm over here!'

Justin turned around and saw Sam in the middle of a group of people.

15 'Come and look at this,' shouted Sam as he waved to Justin. 'It's really cool.'

Justin walked over to Sam.

'Hi Sam,' he said quietly. 'What's going on?'

'Just wait a second,' said Sam.

20 In front of them was a very strange statue of Sir Francis Drake – the famous ship captain. He left from Plymouth harbour in 1577 to sail around the world. Justin looked at the statue. Sam was right. It was cool and bit scary. The sea captain was gold from head to toe. Justin took his video
25 camera out of his bag and turned it on.

'This is interesting,' he thought.

A big seagull landed on the statue's head. It looked at the group of people. A girl, with a red T-shirt with a picture of a big lion's head on it, walked up to the statue. The
30 seagull looked down at the girl as she put some coins into the gold box in front of the statue. For a moment nothing

happened and everybody was very quiet. Suddenly the statue moved one of its hands! What a shock! The seagull flew away. Then 'Sir Francis Drake' quickly took off his gold hat to thank the girl. Everybody clapped and laughed.

5   'How could that statue stand like that for so long and not move?' Sam asked Justin as they walked along the street.

    'I don't know. It was really cool. He didn't even move when the seagull sat on his head,' said Justin.

10   'Yeah, that was really funny.'

    The two boys laughed.

    'So how did you know about the jumble sale?' Justin asked Sam.

    'Somebody gave Dad a flyer about it when he went to

15 the supermarket.'

    Justin was surprised.

    'Your dad goes to the supermarket?' he asked.

    'Yes, he usually does the shopping,' said Sam. 'It's great because he always buys interesting things. When mum

20 does the shopping it's so boring.'

    Justin was very quiet. 'I wonder if Dad is going to the supermarket in Boston today,' he thought.

CHAPTER 2

Some minutes later Justin and Sam arrived at the jumble sale. There were red, white and blue flags over the big front door. It was open, and there was a very big poster next to it:

5

WELCOME TO OUR JUMBLE SALE!
Come in and look around.
All the money you spend is for the
Good Dog Rescue Centre.
Make a dog happy today!

10 A man in a dog costume stood at the door.

'Woof, woof,' he said to the boys as he waved his long tail with his hand. 'Dogs with their people can come in for free, or it's a pound for people without dogs.'

Sam looked at Justin.

15 'Er … what do you think? I didn't know we …'

Suddenly a brown dog ran to the man in the dog costume and started to bark loudly.

'So what's your problem little dog?' laughed the man.

'Skip, be quiet!' said a girl's voice. 'Now!'

20 The brown dog stopped barking and the two boys turned around. There was Abby.

'Hello guys,' she said.

'Hi,' said Justin and Sam.

Abby smiled and then she looked at the man in the dog
25 costume. 'I'm really sorry about my dog,' she said to him.

'No problem. All the dogs bark at me,' he said. 'Are these two boys with you?

'Yes,' said Abby.

'OK,' said the man. 'You and your friends can go in for free because you have a dog.'

He waved his tail again and Abby smiled at him. Sam and Justin smiled at Abby.

'I'm surprised to see you here,' whispered Abby to the boys. 'I thought jumble sales are a girl's thing.'

'Ha, ha', said Sam.

'Yeah, we … er …,' said Justin.

Sam looked at his friend and said quickly, 'It was my idea because Justin needs to buy a birthday present. What are you doing here?'

'Mum helped to prepare the jumble sale, and I want to help her make the sandwiches,' said Abby. 'Maya is here, too – her mum is selling some things. I have to take Skip for a walk now so see you later.'

'OK,' Sam said. 'Come on, Justin let's go in and have a look around.'

When they were inside, Justin was surprised. He could see lots of tables and the things on them looked very interesting. There were lots of people, and lots of dogs, too.

'This is going to be fun,' he thought.

'Where's that terrible music coming from?' said Sam.

'Er … over there,' said Justin.

He pointed to the stage. There was a woman with a piano. She also wore a funny dog costume.

'Maybe she's married to the man at the door,' laughed Sam.

Two girls stood next to the piano and sang a song called 'You're a good dog'. Nobody really listenend to them; everybody was too busy and more interested in what was on the tables.

5 The two boys also started to look at some of the things people were selling.

'What's this?' said Justin as he took something from one of the tables. 'Is it for CDs or something?'

'Oh, you put toast in it and then you put it on the table,' said Sam. 'We have one at home.'

'That's silly,' said Justin. 'Mum just puts the toast on a plate'. Then he saw something really interesting.

'Wow, look at this old camera!' he said excitedly.

'How do you know it's old?' asked Sam.

15 'It's not digital. It uses film. I could take some cool photos with this. And it's cheap. It's only eight pounds, and I have ten pounds,' said Justin as he started to take some money out of his pocket.

'Er … what about the birthday present. Remember?' asked Sam.

'Oh, yeah, I almost forgot,' said Justin. 'You're right.'

He put the money back in his pocket. Just then Abby and Skip stood next to the boys. Abby was eating a big cupcake and Skip was looking at it.

25 'No, this isn't for you,' laughed Abby. 'Cupcakes are not good for dogs.'

'Wow, where did you get that from?' Sam asked her. 'It looks really cool.'

'It tastes good, too,' said Abby. 'Maya's mum made it. 30 She's selling them on her table. Come on. Let's go there.'

There were lots of people in front of the table where Maya and her mum had their cupcakes and other stuff.

'Hi Maya' said Abby. 'Look. I think they want one of your famous cupcakes. I have to find mum so see you later.'

'OK. Hi guys,' said Maya.

'Hi, Maya,' said Sam. 'Your cupcakes are selling fast.'

'Yes, are you worried?' laughed Maya. She took two big cupcakes from the table and gave them to the boys.

'You don't have to pay for them,' she whispered. 'But don't tell anybody.'

'Wow, this is yummy,' said Justin as he started to eat.

'The best cupcake …,' said Sam with his mouth full.

There was also a little old lady near the table. She had a big cupcake in her hand.

'Hm, I love cupcakes,' she said.

She took a big bite out of her cupcake and said, 'Thith ith tho goodh buth a bith thewthy'.

The old lady was hard to understand. Then Justin knew why as he looked at her mouth.

'Where are her teeth?' thought Justin.

He looked at the rest of her cupcake. What a shock! The little old lady's teeth were still in it! But she wasn't worried. She carefully took the teeth out of the cupcake and tried to put them back in her mouth.

Sam started to laugh but Justin quickly pulled him away. They almost hit a tall woman. She had a cup of tea in her hand.

'Watch where you're going?' she said angrily. 'This tea is very hot and you almost …'

'Sorry,' said Sam. 'We didn't see you.'

'Yeah, sorry,' said Justin.

The woman looked at them with her cold dark black eyes. She didn't say a word. The boys watched her as she walked away.

'She's very strange,' said Sam.

5 'Yeah, and scary,' said Justin. 'Her face is so white. She looks like a vampire.'

'She isn't a vampire because vampires don't drink tea, and they don't go to jumbles sales,' said Sam.

The two boys looked at each other.

10 'Or maybe they do …,' said Justin quietly.

CHAPTER 3

There was a loud sound coming from the stage in the jumble sale. The man in the dog costume had the microphone in his hand.

'One two three,' he said as he hit it. 'Woof woof woof? 15 Can you hear me?'

'YES!' somebody shouted.

'Good,' he said. 'I'd like to say something very important. Please don't forget to buy tickets for our raffle today. You can win some great prizes. Just have a look at 20 them on the raffle table in front of the stage. All the money you spend on the tickets is for the Good Dog Rescue …'

Suddenly there was a loud scream. A small black and white dog ran onto the stage with a big cupcake in its mouth. Another dog ran after it. Everybody laughed and 25 clapped as the dogs ran off the stage.

'Er, yes, those cupcakes are really good,' said the man in the dog costume. 'Well, the raffle is in about 30 minutes, so please come and look at the prizes. There are still tickets but not many! Thank you.'

As the man in the dog costume walked off the stage he almost fell over his tail. Everybody laughed at him. But one woman didn't laugh. She looked at her watch with her cold black eyes.

Sam and Justin didn't know what to do when suddenly Lucy was next to them.

'Hi guys,' she said.

'Hi Lucy,' said the boys together.

'Maya didn't tell us that you're here,' said Sam.

Lucy looked sad, and then she looked angry.

'I'm not talking to her,' she said.

'What happened?' asked Justin.

'I looked at the stuff on her table and I saw a book about sailing boats. I gave her that book for her birthday and now she's selling it!' said Lucy.

'Oh,' said Sam. He could see that Lucy was really sad.

'Is it really the same book?' he asked.

'Yes,' said Lucy. 'But I don't want to talk about it.'

'We're going to look at the raffle table, said Sam.

'Are we?' asked Justin surprised.

'Yes,' said Sam as he gave Justin a small kick on his leg.

'Er … oh, yes we are,' said Justin.

'Do you want to come with us?' said Sam.

'OK,' said Lucy. 'That's a good idea.'

When the three kids found the raffle table, the man with the dog costume was there.

'Only a pound for five tickets and look at these great prizes you can win,' he said as he pointed to the things on the table. 'Some of the big prizes are maybe interesting for you: a trip to Butterfly World, skates, an e-book reader, photo computer software …'

'That photo software is cool,' said Justin. 'It's very expensive in the shops.'

'… And there are also some smaller prizes: DVDs, chocolates, dog biscuits …' said the man in the dog costume.

Lucy pointed to an interesting box with lions on it and asked, 'Are there jewels and gold in there?'

'No,' there's nothing in it,' laughed the man in the dog costume as he opened the box. 'But you can put gold and jewels in it. It's one of the big prizes because it's very old.'

Sam looked at the box too.

'Yes, you're right Lucy,' he said. 'It is interesting, and it looks like a sea captain's chest. What do you think Justin?'

'I'd like to buy five tickets,' said Justin.

'What do you think about the box?' said Sam.

But Justin was busy trying to find his money in his pocket.

'Would you like a strip of gold, red, or blue tickets? I have only these three strips now,' said the man in the dog costume.

'Gold, please,' said Justin. 'What about you guys? Are you going to buy some tickets, too?'

'Yes, OK,' said Sam. 'A strip of red tickets for me, please.'

'So I'd like the blue tickets, please,' said Lucy. 'A pound isn't much.'

'That's right and the money is for the …'

'Good Dog Rescue Centre!' said the three kids together.

The man in the dog costume laughed and said, 'Great. Now I don't have any more tickets.'

He looked at his watch.

'It's time to start the raffle!'

5   Just then the woman with the cold black eyes came and sat near the raffle table. She had a lot of raffle tickets, all different colours. Suddenly her mobile rang and she quickly answered it.

'Yes, it's about to start,' the woman said quietly. 'No, 10 don't worry. I want the box and I'll get it.'

CHAPTER 4

The man in the dog costume ran onto the stage with a big red box in his hand.

'Ladies and gentlemen, children, and er ... dogs of course. May I have your attention, please?'

15   He quickly looked at the two girls on the stage. This time they didn't sing. They started to play big trumpets. It sounded important, like something you hear when the Queen of England comes into the room! Nobody spoke because the trumpets were so loud, but all the dogs 20 howled. When the girls finished, Justin and Sam took their fingers out of their ears and two or three people clapped.

'I think only the girls' parents clapped,' whispered Sam to Justin. The two boys laughed.

'I heard what you just said,' whispered Lucy. 'It's not 25 easy to play a trumpet in front of lots of people.'

Sam and Justin's faces went a bit red.

'Thank you,' said the man in the dog costume. 'OK, the big moment of the jumble sale is here. It's time for the raffle! I'm going to start with the smaller prizes first. When you hear me call your number, come up to the raffle table and choose a prize. My assistant, she looks a bit like me, will help you.'

The woman in the dog costume behind the raffle table, waved her tail. On the stage, the man in the dog costume put his hand into his big red box and pulled out a ticket. He looked at it and then spoke slowly into the microphone.

'The first winning ticket is blue, number one hundred and forty five. One-four-five.'

'You have blue tickets,' Sam said to Lucy.

'Yes, but not one-four-five,' she said.

'Over here,' shouted a girl from the back.

'Our first winner,' said the man in the dog costume.

Justin, Sam and Lucy watched Maya go to the raffle table with a blue ticket in her hand.

'Ah, a box of dog biscuits, a good prize to choose,' said the man in the dog costume as he watched her chose her prize.

'Hmmm, Maya doesn't have a dog,' said Justin.

'No, but Abby does,' said Lucy. She looked very sad.

'Come on,' said Sam. 'There are lots more prizes.'

'Red thirteen. One-three,' said the man in the dog costume from the stage.

This time, nobody shouted 'over here'. The man in the dog costume scratched one of his big dog ears.

'Check your tickets,' he said. 'Who has red thirteen?'

'Maybe the winner is at home watching the football on TV,' a man shouted.

A lot of people laughed.

'Don't worry, you can watch the game later.' laughed the man in the dog costume. Then he looked at the woman with dark eyes. 'Excuse me Madam. I think you have red thirteen. Am I right?'

5 The tall woman looked at all the red tickets she had in her hand and then slowly stood up. She walked over to the table, chose a DVD and then sat down again.

'So vampires like raffles,' whispered Sam into Justin's ear. 'Look at all those tickets she has.'

10 'Vampires are very rich,' whispered Justin.

'Do you think she chose the Dracula DVD?' Sam smiled.

'Shhhh, or we'll miss our numbers,' said Lucy.

'It doesn't matter,' said Justin. 'I never win anything.'

'You never know what's going to happen,' whispered
15 Sam in Justin's ear as Lucy gave them another angry look.

The man in the dog costume read out more numbers and soon all of the smaller prizes on the raffle table were gone.

'And now it's time for the big prizes,' he said excitedly
20 'The first one is a day trip for all the family to Butterfly World. And, the lucky winner for this great prize is blue three hundred and eight. Three-oh-eight blue.'

'I wonder if the vampire has that ticket, too. She's winning most of the prizes,' said Justin. 'It's not fair.'

25 'She isn't even looking at her tickets,' said Sam.

'Over here!' a man shouted.

'Well, she didn't win that prize,' said Justin.

'Good for the butterflies,' laughed Sam. 'We all know that vampires like to eat …'

30 'Our next prize is for a clever computer expert …'

'Shhhhh,' said Justin. He was very excited. Sam looked at Lucy. She smiled.

'… It's professional photo software. And the winning ticket for this really nice prize is gold …'

Justin looked at his strip of five gold tickets. 'I can feel this is going to be my lucky day,' he thought.

5   'Good luck Justin,' whispered Lucy.

'… And the number is nine hundred and sixty-nine; nine-six-nine.'

Justin looked at his tickets again. His mouth fell open but no words came out. His face was white.

10   Sam took Justin's tickets and looked at them. 'That's your number, Justin!'

'Oh no, wait a moment,' said the man in the dog costume. 'I am very sorry. I made a mistake. The number is six hundred and ninety six. Six-nine-six. I am really very
15   sorry about that.'

Justin's face suddenly went red.

'Oh, that's really bad luck, Justin,' said Sam.

'Yes, why isn't that silly man more careful?' said Lucy.

'I told you I never win anything,' said Justin.

20   'Oh no …' said Sam quietly. 'Look. The vampire won it!'

The three kids watched as the tall woman with the black eyes went back to her chair again and put the software prize into her big black bag.

25   'She looks like she thinks it's boring to win so many prizes,' said Justin. 'I want to go home now.'

'But the raffle isn't over yet,' said Sam.

'Sam's right,' said Lucy.

'OK,' said Justin.

The man in the dog costume read out more numbers and the winners collected their prizes. Then there was only one prize left on the raffle table.

'And now,' he said. 'We come to the last prize in the raffle today – the beautiful box with the lions on it.'

'I hope somebody nice wins it,' whispered Lucy. 'Not your vampire.'

The three kids looked at the tall woman. She stood next to the raffle table and looked at the man in the dog costume.

'That's strange,' said Justin. 'She's interested in the raffle now, and her eyes have a strange light in them.'

'Yes, you're right,' said Sam slowly. 'I don't like her. I don't like her at all …'

'I hate her,' said Justin.

The man in the dog costume pulled a ticket out of his red box.

'The winner of the box with the lions on it is nine hundred and sixty-nine; nine-six-nine. Er … we had this number before, didn't we?' he said as he scratched one of his big ears again.

'That was another number,' shouted somebody. 'What's the colour of this one?'

'Oh sorry, it's gold. Gold nine-six-nine.'

Justin looked at his ticket. This time there was no mistake.

'Over here!' he quickly shouted.

'You won it,' shouted Lucy excitedly.

'Good, we have a young winner over there,' said the man in the dog costume.

'See, I told you,' Sam said as he hit Justin on his back.

'Yes, but …' said Justin.

'Go on,' said Sam. 'Go and get your prize.'

Justin walked to the raffle table and gave his gold ticket to the woman in the dog costume.

'You're a very lucky boy,' she said as she gave him the box with the lions on it.

'Er … thank you,' said Justin.

He went back to his friends. They smiled at him.

'I'm so happy you won it and not her,' said Lucy.

The three kids looked at the tall woman. Her face was even whiter than before. She looked at Justin for a moment with her sad dark eyes, and then she took her mobile out of her pocket and started to speak into it.

CHAPTER 5

Justin looked at his prize and touched the lions on it with his finger.

'What am I going to do with this box?' he said.

'It could be a nice present for your grandma,' said Sam.

'Yes, it's so beautiful and mysterious,' said Lucy. 'And it's old. Old people like old things.'

'Maybe you're right,' said Justin. 'These lions are …'

Suddenly the tall woman with the dark eyes was in front of him. He almost dropped the box with shock.

'So you won the box,' said the cold voice.

'What's it to you?' said Justin. He was trying not to sound too nervous.

'It's not a very interesting prize for a boy like you,' said the tall woman. 'Maybe you like computers. Here's something to think about. Give me the box and you can have the computer software I won.'

Justin and the other two kids watched her take the photo software out of her big black bag.

'You can't do much with your prize,' she said as she slowly waved the software in front of Justin.

'Er … no I can't,' said Justin slowly.

'Yes, you can!' said Sam quickly. He gave Justin a hard kick. 'Remember your grandmother!'

'Ouch,' said Justin.

'Don't give it to her, Justin,' said Lucy quietly.

'Let your friend talk for himself,' said the tall woman. Her eyes were even darker now. 'Well?'

Justin looked at her. He felt like she wanted to pull him down into a very dark and dangerous place.

'I have a better idea,' said the tall woman. 'What about I give you the photo software and ten pounds? Then you can buy your grandmother a really nice present.'

Justin looked down at the lions on the box. They were looking at him like they were saying: 'Please don't let her take us away. We want to stay with you.'

He looked into the black eyes and said slowly: 'No. I want to keep the box.'

'Good,' whispered Lucy to Sam.

'Fifteen pounds,' said the tall woman.

'No,' said Justin again. He held the box close to him.

'Twenty pounds,' said the tall woman.

Justin's face went red. 'Twenty pounds was a lot of money,' he thought. He started to feel sick as the tall woman's face got near to his.

Suddenly there was a loud sound from the stage. The man in the dog costume spoke into the microphone on the stage again. This time he looked very serious.

'Excuse me, ladies and gentlemen. Can I have your attention? There is a dark green Jaguar parked in the fire exit. Somebody is going to phone the police in one minute. If it's your car, please move it now before it's too late!'

Suddenly the tall woman put the software back into her bag. She gave Justin one last look and said coldly, 'Think about it. We will meet again, and very soon.'

The three kids watched her as she walked away very quickly.

'Wow, you were so cool,' said Lucy.

'Was I?' said Justin. 'She was scary.'

'Yes, but you were really cool,' said Sam.

'I wonder why she wants your box so much?' asked Lucy.

'Good question,' said Justin. Suddenly his mobile beeped.

R U still at jumble sale? Do U want me 2 pick U up? XOX mum

'Oh, it's Mum,' said Justin. 'I just have to quickly text her back.'

Yes please ☺

His mobile beeped again.

OK R U ready now?

'Are you in trouble?' asked Lucy.

'I don't think so,' said Justin as he answered his mum's text.

Yes When can U b here?

'She can pick me up with the car. That's great because
5 then I don't have to walk all the way home with this box.'

'Cool, I hope you told her not to park in the fire exit,' laughed Sam.

Suddenly Justin looked worried.

'What's the matter,' asked Sam.

10 'Do you think the vampire is still outside,' asked Justin. 'Maybe she's waiting for me to come out.'

'We'll come out with you,' said Sam.

'Yes, of course,' said Lucy. 'So don't worry,'

'But I am worried,' said Justin. 'Remember what she
15 said!'

'How is she going to find you?' said Sam. 'She doesn't even know who you are or where you live.'

Justin looked worried again.

'Do you guys want to come to my place now?' he said.

20 'OK,' said Sam. 'What about your mum?'

'Yes, Sam's right,' said Lucy. 'Maybe you should ask her first.'

'She's always happy when friends visit me,' said Justin. 'But I'll ask her.'

25 Justin's phone beeped again.

'Oh, maybe it's the vampire this time,' laughed Sam.

On my way. C U outside

'Ha, ha. No, it's mum,' said Justin as he texted back.

Gr8 ☺ Can my friends Sam and Lucy come 2?

'It's OK,' said Justin. 'Let's go and wait for her.'

The three kids made their way through the jumble sale to the front door. Suddenly Justin stopped and looked at Sam in a nervous way.

'Oh, er … I see,' said Sam. 'OK, you guys wait here.'

One minute later Sam came back to them.

'Well?' asked Justin.

'I can't see the vampire,' said Sam.

'What about her car?' asked Lucy.

'There's no sign of her green Jaguar in the fire exit, so the coast is clear.'

'Great,' said Justin. 'Come on.'

Justin and Lucy followed Sam outside. Just then they heard a car horn. It was Justin's mum.

'Hi guys,' she shouted. 'Jump in. I'm not allowed to park in the fire exit.'

The kids quickly got in: Sam and Lucy in the back, and Justin in the front.

'Hello, Mrs Skinner,' said Sam and Lucy together.

'Good to see you, Mum,' said Justin as he closed his door. 'OK, let's go!'

His mother smiled and started the car.

Justin looked down at the box in his hands. The lions looked like they were happy.

CHAPTER 6

'Did you all have a good time at the jumble sale?' asked Justin's mum as she stopped the car at a red light.

'Yes, thank you, Mrs Skinner,' said Sam from the back of the car.

5 'The best thing was that Justin won a really cool prize in the raffle,' Lucy said.

Justin's mum smiled.

Justin's face was a bit red.

'The tickets weren't expensive, Mum,' he said quickly. 10 'I only spent a pound.'

'That's all right, love. It's your pocket money and you can spend it on what you like. What did you win?'

'This box,' said Justin. 'I think it's a nice birthday present for Grandma.'

15 Mrs Skinner quickly looked at the box in Justin's hands. 'It looks very old. I'm sure she will love it,' she said.

The light turned green and the car moved again.

'Grandma sends you lots of love,' said Justin's mum.

'Thanks,' said Justin as he touched the lions again with 20 his finger.

His mother looked in the rear-view mirror.

'I hope you two like chocolate cake,' she said to Sam and Lucy. 'Justin's grandmother gave me a big one. She made it yesterday, so we can all have some of it for tea.'

25 'That sounds great, Mrs Skinner,' said Lucy from the back of the car.

'My dad can make cakes,' said Sam. 'They're really good. He learned how to make them in the Navy. They look like those cakes you see in magazines. Mum tried to make a cake once …'

'Only once?' said Lucy.

'Yes, once was enough,' laughed Sam. 'When she took
it out of the oven it was black and hard. We couldn't eat it. She never made another cake!'

Lucy started to laugh. Justin looked at his mother as she started to laugh too. He tried to smile but he felt sad. He looked out of the window.

'I don't even know if Dad can make cakes,' he thought. 'Maybe he makes them in Boston, but I don't think so because he never has much time. He always works …'

Suddenly there was a loud car horn. His mother looked in the rear-view mirror again.

'Silly person,' she said. 'I'm trying to park and she almost crashed into us. Some people think the road is just for them. They are all the same – those Jaguar drivers.'

Justin's face went white. He quickly turned around to look out of the back window. Lucy and Sam did the same. But there was no sign of a Jaguar.

'What colour was it, Mum?'

'Green. It went around the corner.'

Justin looked at Sam and Lucy. They didn't say a word. Mrs Skinner stopped the car.

'So here we are,' she said.

Justin said nothing.

'Are you OK, love?' said his mother. 'You look tired.'

He looked down at the box.

'Well, a nice piece of grandma's cake and a drink is what you need,' said his mum brightly as she opened the door of the car. 'Come on, everybody. Let's go inside!'

'Mum, is it OK if we go into my room?' said Justin when they were all inside the house.

'Yes, of course, love. I'll prepare your drinks and cake.'

'Thanks. Come on guys.'

5 Justin went with his two friends upstairs. The three kids sat on the floor in Justin's room and he put the box in front of them.

'Do you think it was the vampire?' he said.

'Maybe your mum didn't see a Jaguar but another kind
10 of car,' said Lucy.

'But it was green,' said Sam.

'A frog is green,' said Lucy.

'Ha ha,' said Sam. 'But what I don't understand is why she wanted the box.'

15 'It's very old,' said Lucy. 'So maybe she knows she can sell it and get a lot of money for it, maybe five hundred pounds or more.'

'Do you think the lions are gold?' said Justin as he touched them with his finger. 'I think they are.'

20 'Maybe it's a magic box and that's why your vampire wants it,' said Lucy. 'Maybe she knows the secret of this box and she'll live for five hundred years, or never die.'

'I wonder what the secret of this box is,' said Justin as he opened it and carefully looked inside.

25 Suddenly they heard Justin's mum knock on the door of his room.

'Can I come in, love?' said his mother.

'Er… just a minute,' said Justin.

He quickly closed the box, stood up and put it on his
30 desk. Then he opened the door.

'Here are your drinks and some of grandma's cake,' said his mother.

'Thanks, Mum.'

'Yes, thanks Mrs Skinner,' said Sam and Lucy.

'Don't you want to sit on chairs?' asked Mrs Skinner. 'It's not very comfortable on the floor.'

5 'We're fine, Mum,' said Justin.

'OK. Well, just come downstairs when you need something more to eat or drink.'

'OK, Mum,' said Justin as his mother left the room. He closed the door again.

10 'This cake looks really good,' said Lucy.

'Yes,' said Justin as he sat down on the floor.

The three kids ate and drank. They didn't say much. After a minute or two, Sam spoke first.

'I have an idea,' he said suddenly. He was excited.

15 'What?' said Justin and Lucy together.

'Let's go to the museum tomorrow,' said Sam. 'There are lots of old things there and maybe there is an old box like this one. Then we can find out more about it.'

'That's a great idea,' said Lucy. 'But I don't think the 20 museum is open on Sundays.'

She looked at her mobile.

'No, it's only open from Tuesday to Saturday. I can't go on Tuesday because I'm going to visit my grandparents on their farm.'

25 'I can come to the museum,' said Justin. 'I'll take the box with me'.

'Cool,' said Sam. 'We have a plan. I think I have to go home now.'

'Yes, me too,' said Lucy. 'It's getting late.'

30 'I'm sorry you can't come with us, Lucy,' said Justin.

'Me, too, but tell me what you find out,' said Lucy.

'Of course,' said Justin.

He stood up and quickly looked out of the window. Suddenly his face went white.

'Look!' he said.

Sam and Lucy looked out of the window too. A green Jaguar drove past the house.

'Was it her?' said Sam.

'I don't know,' said Justin. 'I couldn't see.'

Lucy looked very serious.

'Maybe it's a good idea if you don't take the box to the museum,' she said. 'And I think you should stay at home until Tuesday. Don't go outside.'

Justin looked at Lucy and then at Sam.

'Yes,' said Sam quietly. 'I think Lucy's right.'

CHAPTER 7

On Tuesday it rained. Justin met Sam outside Plymouth City Museum and Art Gallery. Sam almost didn't know it was Justin because Justin wore a very big rain hat and a big rain coat.

'Are you trying to hide yourself from the rain or from the vampire?' said Sam. 'Did you see the Jaguar again?'

'No, but I didn't really look. I stayed in my room all the time and did stuff on my computer. Mum just thought I was a bit sick, so it was OK.'

'Good,' said Sam. 'Come on, let's get out of this rain.'

They went inside the museum. There was a man behind a big desk. He smiled at them.

'Hello,' he said. 'Can I help you?'

'Er … we want to look at old boxes,' said Justin. 'Do you have any here?'

'Oh yes, we have a lot of old tea chests, jewel boxes and porcelain boxes from China upstairs,' said the man.

5 Then he pointed to a big door behind him.

'And through that door we have also lots of fascinating objects. You can also learn about life and death in Egypt. There are many different old boxes in that part of the museum too. There are also some tables. You can sit and
10 read or do activities.'

'Thanks,' said Justin. 'That sounds like what we are looking for.'

'Could we have two tickets, please?' asked Sam. The friendly man smiled again.

15 'You don't have to pay. This museum is free,' he said.

'Really?' said Justin. 'That's great.'

The man pointed to a smaller room.

'Please put your wet coats in there. Then you can have a look around.'

20 The two boys ran upstairs. The first thing they saw was a big glass display case. They looked at the old boxes from China in it.

'Interesting,' said Sam as he read the small information card next to one of the boxes. 'It says here that these boxes
25 are tea caddies.'

'They are beautiful,' said Justin. 'Why did people in those days make such special boxes to keep tea in?'

'Dad told me a bit about the history of tea.' said Sam. 'It was really expensive five hundred years ago, and only rich
30 people drank it. It came from China to Europe in ships, and then some Queen started drinking it here in England

and then everybody started drinking it – well, the rich people. Of course it's cheap now.'

'My mum likes green tea,' said Justin. 'I don't like it.'

'Wow, this box is from 1580,' said Sam. 'It has some lions on it. Are they like your lions?'

Justin took his mobile out of his pocket.

'I can check. I took some photos of my box.'

The two boys looked at Justin's photos very carefully.

'Hmmm,' said Sam. 'They look like your lions, but the box is very different.'

'If the lions are the same, maybe my box is about six hundred years old too. But you're right. It's not a tea … er … what did you call it?'

'A tea caddy,' said Sam. 'There are more boxes and things in those display cases over there.'

The two boys started to walk around and look at the other mysterious objects in the room.

'Wow, that's really ugly,' said Justin as he looked at a porcelain figure of a strange old fat man.

Sam stood next to Justin and read the card that was in front of the figure.

'It's to put tobacco in,' said Sam.

But Justin didn't listen to Sam. He looked worried.

'What's wrong?' asked Sam. 'Are you …?'

'Shhhh,' said Justin. 'Can you hear that?'

'What? It's just someone talking downstairs,' said Sam.

'I know that voice,' said Justin. 'Come on.'

Justin walked quickly and quietly to the top of the stairs. Sam followed him. Justin's face went white. The nice man at the desk was talking to a tall woman.

'Look, it's her,' whispered Justin. 'I knew it.'

'Are you sure?' whispered Sam. 'We can't really see her face.'

Suddenly the woman turned around and looked up the stairs with her dark eyes. Justin and Sam quickly sat on the floor next to the big display case.

'You're right,' whispered Sam. 'It's the vampire. Do you think she saw us?'

'Shhhh, let's listen to what they are saying …'

'I'm happy you found what you wanted,' said the man.

'Yes, thank you.' said the woman. 'Well, it's good the rain stopped. I hate it. Good bye.'

'Good bye, Madam,' said the man.

Justin and Sam stood up very slowly and watched the woman leave the museum.

'That was scary,' said Justin. 'What did she want?'

'Maybe she was just looking at the objects from Egypt, and about death and mummies,' said Sam with a bit of a smile. 'Vampires are interested in all that stuff.'

Justin wasn't smiling.

'She saw something in that room downstairs,' he said. 'Maybe she found out something about the box. We have to find out what.'

'But she already knows more about the box than we do. That's why she wants it,' said Sam.

'Yes, and we have to find out what its secret is before she finds us,' said Justin.

'Yes,' said Sam. 'So let's look in the room downstairs.'

Sam started to go down the stairs but Justin wasn't moving. Sam turned around and looked at his friend.

'Come on, Justin. What are you waiting for?'

Justin looked very worried.

'Do you think the vampire's going to come back?'

'No,' said Sam. 'Why is she going to come back to this museum today?'

'I don't know,' said Justin. 'I just have a strange feeling.'

'Don't worry,' said Sam. 'You watch too many horror films. Come on!'

CHAPTER 8

'Wow, it's really dark in here,' said Justin.

'Yes,' said Sam. 'This old stuff doesn't like the light. Just like vampires.'

The two boys walked past a coffin that looked like an Egyptian pharaoh. It was following them with its eyes.

'Is there really a mummy in there?' said Justin.

'No, but maybe the vampire is sleeping in it,' laughed Sam. 'Wow, look at all these little figures. It says here that they're magic and come to life to help the dead person.'

'I think the Egyptians were really cool,' said Justin. 'I wonder if there's life after you die.'

'I hope so,' said Sam. 'But I still want to play basketball in the afterlife or do kung fu.'

'Maybe in the afterlife I can see my dad all the time.'

'I don't want to see my little sister all the time,' said Sam. 'Scary! Come on, let's look in there.'

The two boys went into the next room. Suddenly Sam saw something very interesting in one of the display cases.

'Look at this,' he said. 'It's a box for jewels, and it's a bit like your box.'

Justin looked at the box through the glass. The box was open and it looked broken, but Justin suddenly understood why, and he was very excited.

'Look,' he said. 'When you put a nail or something in that small hole you can take out part of the box and there's a secret drawer.'

Sam looked at Justin.

'Are you thinking what I am thinking?' said Sam.

'I think so,' said Justin. 'Let's go back to my place and look at my box again. Maybe it has a …'

Suddenly someone sneezed very loudly. Sam and Justin almost fell on the floor with shock. They turned around and saw a girl sitting at a table making something with small pieces of coloured paper. She wore a red T-shirt with a big lion's head on it, yellow jeans and gold trainers.

'That's strange,' thought Justin. 'I know that T-shirt but where did …?'

The girl looked at Justin. Her eyes were bright blue, like a lake in summer. He walked over to her.

'Er … where are you going, Justin?' said Sam. 'I thought you wanted to …'

But Justin stood next to the girl.

'Hello,' he said.

'Hello,' said the girl. 'I'm sorry I was so loud.'

'That's OK,' said Justin.

Then Sam came over and stood next to Justin.

'Yeah, you almost woke up the pharaoh,' he said.

The girl smiled at Sam and then looked at Justin.

'Er … I'm Justin, and this is my friend Sam.'

'I'm Poppy,' said the girl.

Justin looked at the small box Poppy was making with the coloured paper.

'Cool,' he said. 'You're really good at that.'

'Thanks,' said Poppy. 'My dad showed me how to make origami animals and other things. I miss him a lot. He died last year but I always feel he's looking at me when I do it.'

'Oh,' said Justin. 'I'm sorry about your dad. It looks very difficult.'

Poppy smiled at him.

'Not when you know how. I'll show you how to do it.'

'That's nice,' said Sam quickly. 'But we have to go.'

Justin looked at Sam and then at Poppy.

'Er … that's right,' he said. 'Could you show me later?'

'Of course,' said Poppy. 'Just give me your mobile number or something, and I'll text you.'

'Cool,' said Justin as he quickly wrote his number on a small piece of paper. 'Don't forget.'

'No,' said Poppy. 'Bye.'

'Mum isn't home,' said Justin as he opened the front door. 'She's still at work.'

The two boys ran into Justin's room. He went over to a small cupboard next to his bed and took out the box.

'So, let's see if it has a secret drawer like the one in the museum,' said Justin as he put the box on the desk.

He turned on the light, held up the box under it and opened it.

'Look,' said Justin excitedly. 'There's a small hole!'

'Wow, you're right,' said Sam. 'It's very hard to see.'

'Hold the box for a second,' said Justin. 'I think a paper clip will help us.' He took one from his desk.

Very carefully, Justin pushed one end of the paper clip into the small hole. Suddenly the piece of wood with the hole in it came off, and Justin and Sam could see a small secret drawer. They looked at each other.

'Maybe there's nothing in the drawer,' said Justin.

'Well, just have a look! What are you waiting for?' said Sam.

Justin slowly opened the secret drawer and his mouth opened with shock. There WAS something inside. He took it out and looked at it. It was a gold lion with red eyes.

'Wow!' shouted Sam. 'It's a brooch and it's gold. Maybe those red eyes are rubies.'

Justin's face was white. He looked at Sam.

'So maybe the vampire knows that there is a brooch,' said Justin. 'But how, and why …?'

Suddenly Sam's mobile beeped.

'Oh no, it's a text from my dad. I have to go.'

'OK, said Justin. 'Don't tell anybody about this yet.'

'No,' said Sam. 'Don't worry!'

When Sam left, Justin went back upstairs to his room. He looked at the brooch and then at the box. The lions on the box looked happy. Suddenly his phone beeped.

Wanna learn origami 2moro? P oxo

Justin smiled. He carefully put the gold brooch in the box's secret drawer and put it back in the cupboard next to his bed. Then he started to write a text to Poppy.

The house Poppy lived in was just around the corner from Justin's, and it looked like his. She opened the door to let him in.

'It's cool you live so near,' she said. 'Come in. I'm going to have some green tea,' said Poppy. 'Would you like some?'

'Er … OK,' said Justin.

He followed her into the kitchen. Poppy made two cups of tea and gave one to Justin. He drank some of it.

'This tea's nice,' said Justin. 'My mum drinks green tea too, but this is better. I don't know why.'

'My dad always said it's good for me,' said Poppy.

Justin thought of his dad. He felt happy to see him in the summer holidays. Then suddenly he remembered something.

'I saw you on Saturday. You gave the statue some money and you wore the same T-shirt.'

'You're right,' smiled Poppy. 'It's my favourite.'

'Sam and I watched him before we went to a jumble sale near there.'

Suddenly Poppy's blue eyes looked sad.

'Oh,' she said quietly.

'Are you OK?' Justin asked her.

'Yes, I'm fine. Let's go to my room. All the origami paper is up there.'

'I'll show you how to do an easy one first,' said Poppy as they sat at her desk. 'We're going to make a yacht.'

'Great,' said Justin.

Poppy slowly showed Justin what to do, and then he made a yacht. She helped him a little bit, but not much. Then she showed him how to make a diamond.

'You're good at this,' she said.

'It's a lot of fun,' said Justin. 'I'd love to learn how to make more difficult things, too.'

Poppy pointed to a shelf near the window.

'Have a look at those origami animals,' she said. 'They're really difficult to make.'

Justin followed Poppy to the shelf.

'This origami lion is really cool,' said Justin. 'Maybe one day I can make it, too.'

'My father made it. It's my favourite.'

5   Then Poppy showed Justin a photo.

'This is a photo of my father. He's making the lion.'

'Wow,' said Justin.

Justin looked at another photo on the shelf. It was a picture of a woman. Suddenly his face was very white.

10   'Who is this?' he said quietly.

'That's my grandmother,' said Poppy.

Justin didn't say anything. He couldn't stop looking at the photo. The woman in the picture wore a brooch – a gold lion with red eyes.

15   'Are you OK?' asked Poppy.

'Er … yes … I … er …'

Now Justin's face was red. He took his mobile out of his pocket and looked at it.

'It's really late. I have to go,' said Justin as he ran down
20 the stairs. 'I'll send you a text later.'

When Justin got back to his room he called Sam, but there was no answer. He quickly sent Sam a text:

Call me!

Justin looked out of the window and waited. Suddenly
25 he saw a green Jaguar on the street. Justin's face went white. The car stopped outside his house, and the tall woman with the dark eyes got out. She looked up at Justin's window. He quickly sat on the floor so that she couldn't see him.

30   'Come on, Sam! Where are you?' he thought.

CHAPTER 9

The next morning Sam came to Justin's house as soon as he could. Mrs Skinner was at work so the two boys sat in Justin's room with the door open. Justin told Sam everything as they ate chocolate biscuits.

5 'Are you sure it's the same brooch?' said Sam. 'Maybe there are hundreds of them.'

Justin looked at the gold lion with the red eyes he had in his hand.

'I think this brooch is very special,' he said. 'I'm really 10 worried. The vampire knows there's a brooch in the box. Maybe Poppy is in danger.'

Sam looked very serious. So serious, that he stopped eating his chocolate biscuit.

'We don't know she knows about it,' he said.

15 'She knows where I live.'

Sam thought for a second.

'Mum says it's very expensive to park in the town so maybe the vampire wanted to park here. The green Jaguar isn't outside your house now.'

20 'But she looked up at my window?'

'Well, maybe she felt you were looking at her.'

The two boys didn't say anything for a minute or two. Then Justin spoke.

'I think we have to go to Poppy and find out more about 25 her grandmother.'

'WE?' said Sam.

'You always have good ideas,' said Justin. 'Please come with me.'

'Er … OK,' said Sam.

'Thanks, Sam!'
Justin texted Poppy.

Cld I pls C U 2day? W/Sam? Now?

She answered quickly.

5   ☺ **Sure. Now is good**

'Cool, we can go there now,' said Justin. 'I just have to get something from the bathroom'.

'Of course,' said Sam.

One minute later Justin came back into the room with
10   a piece of pink toilet paper. Sam looked at him with a funny look on his face. Justin carefully put the brooch in the toilet paper and then put it in his pocket.

'Ah,' said Sam.

'Right,' said Justin. 'Let's go.'

15   'Aye, aye, captain!'

Sam quickly put the last piece of his chocolate biscuit in his mouth and followed Justin out of the house.

Justin rang the bell on Poppy's front door. Then some seconds later he rang it again.

20   'Are you sure this is the right house?' said Sam.

'Yes, of course,' said Justin.

Just then the door opened and Poppy let them in. She looked a bit tired.

'Hi Poppy,' said Justin.

25   'Hi. Sorry I took so long,' she said. 'So do you want to learn origami too, Sam? Justin's really good at it.'

'Er … yes …' said Sam. 'And I'd love to see your origami animals first. Justin told me about them.'

'Great,' smiled Poppy. 'Let's go to my room. The best ones are there.'

Justin looked at Sam.

'Cool,' said Sam.

5 'Wow, these are beautiful,' said Sam as he and Justin looked at some of the origami animals in Poppy's room.

'Thank you,' said Poppy.

Suddenly there was a loud sound downstairs.

'What was that?' said Justin.

10 'Oh, that's Mum. She went shopping but she's back now. I'll tell her I have some friends here. I'll be back in a minute.'

When Poppy left, Justin showed Sam the photo on the shelf of Poppy's grandmother.

15 'See?' said Justin. 'It's the lion with the red eyes.'

Sam's mouth opened. His face was white.

'It is,' he said slowly.

Just then, Poppy came back into the room.

'Mum has to do some work. She will prepare some food
20 and drink and she says we can make origami in the living room. It's warmer there and the table is big.'

Justin looked at Sam. He didn't say anything. And then Justin looked at Poppy.

'OK,' he said.

25 Poppy was right. It was a big table. She put lots of pieces of coloured paper in the middle of it and then sat in one of the chairs.

'There,' smiled Poppy. 'Let's start.'

'This is fun,' said Justin as he finished an origami bird called a crane.

'A crane is the symbol for a long life and good luck,' said Poppy.

5 Suddenly Justin felt a kick on his leg under the table.

'Go on,' whispered Sam. 'Ask her.'

'Ask me what?' said Poppy.

'I don't know how to ask you this but …'

Justin put his hand in his pocket and pulled out the
10 piece of pink toilet paper and put it on the table.

'Is this something you made?' asked Poppy. 'I'm not sure what it is but …'

'Open it,' said Justin.

Poppy very carefully opened the strange little thing.
15 Then her face went white when she saw what was inside it.

'It's my grandmother's brooch! But how did you …?

'It's a long story,' said Justin. 'And I think you're in danger.'

20 'Why am I in danger?' said Poppy.

Suddenly the living room door opened. Justin and Sam got a shock.

'It's her!' shouted Sam.

The tall woman with the dark eyes was there. In her
25 hand was a big knife.

'Quick, under the table!' shouted Justin. 'She can't get us there.'

The two boys quickly hid under the table. The woman looked at Poppy and came near her.

30 'Come on, Poppy!" shouted Justin from under the table. 'She's going to kill you.'

Poppy put her head under the table and looked at the two boys. They looked very scared.

'What's wrong with you?' she asked quietly. 'This is my mother.'

5 Justin looked at Sam and Sam looked at Justin.

'What? That's your mother? She has a big knife in her hand? Why?'

'She's making some lunch for us,' said Poppy. 'I don't think she's going to kill you. Or me.'

10 'What do you think?' Justin whispered to Sam. 'Do you think it's a trap?'

'I don't know' said Sam.

'Please come out,' said Poppy.

Sam looked at Justin.

15 'OK,' said Justin quietly.

Very slowly Justin and Sam came out from under the table and stood next to Poppy.

'Hello,' said Poppy's mother. She had a shock too.

'You're Poppy's mother?' asked Justin. 'But …'

20 'Yes, I am. You were at the jumble sale and …'

Just then she saw the gold lion with the red eyes on the table. Justin looked at her as she picked it up. Her eyes weren't dark now, they looked nice and friendly.

'You found it in the box, right?' she said.

25 'I think we all need a nice cup of green tea and some chocolate biscuits,' said Poppy. 'And then we can all talk about this.'

'Good idea,' said Justin.

'Very good idea,' said Sam. 'I love chocolate biscuits.'

30 Poppy made the tea, and then her mum told the two boys the story of the box with the lions on it.

'When Poppy's grandmother died, somebody took the box and sold it. When I saw the box at the jumble sale, I was so happy. I called Poppy to tell her the good news. I knew the box had a secret drawer and that the brooch was in it. The brooch is very valuable and …'

Poppy's mum suddenly looked sad.

'It's OK Mum,' said Poppy. 'I'll tell Sam and Justin why we need the money.'

Poppy looked at the two boys.

'I'm sick,' she said. 'I have to go to the USA and then maybe I'll be OK. Mum wanted to sell the brooch to pay for the trip.'

'Oh,' said Justin. 'Now I understand. Well, you have the brooch now and you can sell the box, too.'

Poppy smiled, and then looked at her mum. She was also smiling.

'I want you to keep the box,' said Poppy's mum. 'Do you agree, Poppy?'

'Yes,' said Poppy. 'That's a great idea.'

'Thank you', said Justin. 'I like the box very much. It's very special.'

'Yes, it is' said Sam.

'Good,' said Poppy. 'And I hope you will visit me a lot before I go away. Then you will be almost an origami expert.'

Justin smiled at Poppy.

'Yes,' he said. 'I will.'

Almost every day Justin met Poppy at Poppy's house or at Justin's. Sometimes Sam and Lucy came as well, and sometimes Justin and Poppy's mothers were there, but there were always yummy chocolate biscuits, cake and
5 green tea. The green tea wasn't always hot; sometimes it was nice and cold and had ice in it.

When it was warm, Justin and Poppy made origami in the garden. Justin even made a video of Poppy when she was making a dragon and sent it to his dad. He thought it
10 was really good. The two friends always had a lot of fun and laughed a lot. They sometimes had serious talks, too, when their two mothers weren't around or when Sam and Lucy were busy and had to do other things.

One morning Poppy and Justin sat in the garden alone.
15 Poppy gave Justin a little box.

'This is for you,' she said. 'I'm going to the USA tomorrow.'

Justin was sad. Then he looked at the box.

'It's the origami box you made in the museum,' he said.
20 'Thank you!'

'Open it,' said Poppy.

Justin opened the box and took out an origami lion.

'Is this …?'

'Yes, it's the lion my father made,' said Poppy. 'I want
25 you to have it.'

'It's really cool,' said Justin. 'Thank you.'

He looked at Poppy. She smiled and her eyes were very blue, like a lake in summer.

About two weeks later, two letters from California arrived at Justin's house. One was for his mum and the other was for him. Justin's mum wasn't at home so he put her letter on the kitchen table and opened his. The letter
5 was from Poppy's mum. It was short and sad. In the letter, Poppy's mum told Justin that Poppy was very sick. She had to stay in the USA.

Justin put his letter on the table and slowly made a cup of green tea.

10 'Maybe Mum's letter has the same news,' he thought. 'I'll make her some green tea when she comes home.'

Justin took his tea upstairs to his room. He looked at the box with the lions on it for a very long time, and then he looked at the origami lion next to it.

15 'All the lions look sad, too,' thought Justin.

Suddenly he had an idea.

'I'll put the crane that I made with Poppy in the secret drawer of the box,' he thought. 'Grandma will never know it's there but she will have good luck.'

20 Just then Justin's computer made his favourite sound. His dad in Boston wanted to skype with him. Justin smiled and the lions on the old box and the origami lion smiled, too.

Abbreviations
jm., jn. – jemandem, jemanden; pl – Plural;
sb. – somebody; sth. – something

A
afterlife ['ɑːftəlaɪf] Leben nach
dem Tod
allow [ə'laʊ]: (to) be **(not) allowed
to** (nicht) dürfen
anybody ['enibɒdi] irgendjemand
anything ['eniθɪŋ] irgendetwas
assistant [ə'sɪstənt]
Assistent/in
attention [ə'tenʃn]
Aufmerksamkeit

B
beautiful ['bjuːtɪfl] schön
(to) **beep** [biːp] piepen
best [best]: **the best ones**
die besten
binoculars [bɪ'nɒkjələz] (pl)
Fernglas
broken ['brəʊkən] kaputt
brooch [brəʊtʃ] Brosche

C
car horn ['kɑː ˌhɔːn] Autohupe
chest [tʃest] Truhe
tea chest Teekiste
(to) **clap** [klæp] klatschen
(to) **close** [kləʊz] schließen
close to [kləʊs] dicht bei
coat [kəʊt] Mantel

coast [kəʊst]: **the coast is clear**
die Luft ist rein
coffin ['kɒfɪn] Sarg
coloured ['kʌləd] farbig, bunt
(to) **come off** [ˌkʌm_'ɒf] abfallen
comfortable ['kɒmftəbl]
gemütlich
costume ['kɒstjuːm] Kostüm
crane [kreɪn] Kranich
(to) **crash into sth.** [kræʃ] in etwas
krachen
cupcake ['kʌpkeɪk] Cupcake,
kleiner Kuchen

D
danger ['deɪndʒə] Gefahr
death [deθ] Tod
diamond ['daɪəmənd] Diamant
difficult ['dɪfɪkəlt] schwer,
kompliziert
digital ['dɪdʒɪtl] Digital-
dragon ['drægən] Drache
drawer [drɔː] Fach, Schublade
(to) **drive** [draɪv], **drove**
fahren **driver** Fahrer/in
(to) **drop sth.** [drɒp] etwas fallen
lassen

E

each other [ˌiːtʃ ˈʌðə] einander

Egypt [ˈiːdʒɪpt] Ägypten

Egyptian [ˌiːˈdʒɪpʃn] Ägypter/in, ägyptisch

everything [ˈevriθɪŋ] alles

excuse [ɪkˈskjuːz]: **Excuse me.** Entschuldige./Entschuldigen Sie.

expert [ˈekspɜːt] Experte/ Expertin

F

fascinating [ˈfæsɪneɪtɪŋ] faszinierend

figure [ˈfɪɡə] Figur

(to) **find out** [ˌfaɪnd ˈaʊt] herausfinden

fire exit [ˈfaɪə ˌeksɪt] Notausgang

flag [flæg] Flagge

(to) **fly** [flaɪ], **flew: fly away** wegfliegen

fridge [frɪdʒ] Kühlschrank

front door [ˌfrʌnt ˈdɔː] Eingangstür

G

(to) **get into sth.** [get] in etwas (hinein-)geraten

glass display case [ˌglɑːs ˌdɪˈspleɪ keɪs]: Vitrine, Schaukasten

(to) **go in** [gəʊ] (hinein-)gehen

guy [gaɪ]: **Hi, guys!** Hi, Leute!

H

(to) **happen** [ˈhæpən] passieren, geschehen

hat [hæt] Hut

(to) **hate** [heɪt] hassen

head [hed]: **from head to toe** von Kopf bis Fuß

himself [hɪmˈself]: **for himself** für sich selbst

hole [həʊl] Loch

(to) **howl** [haʊl] heulen, jaulen

I

ice [aɪs] Eis

interested (in) [ˈɪntrəstɪd] interessiert (an)

J

Jaguar [ˈdʒægjuə] *hier:* Jaguar (Automarke)

jewel [ˈdʒuːəl] Juwel

jumble sale [ˈdʒʌmbl ˌseɪl] Trödelmarkt, Wohltätigkeitsbasar

just [dʒʌst]: **just then** genau in diesem Moment

K

(to) **keep** [kiːp] behalten

kick [kɪk] Stoß, Tritt

(to) **kill** [kɪl] töten

knife [naɪf] Messer

(to) **knock** [nɒk]: (to) **knock on** anklopfen

L

lady ['leɪdi] Dame
Ladies and Gentlemen Meine
  Damen und Herren
(to) look [lʊk]: (to) **look around**
  sich umsehen
  (to) **look up** hochschauen,
  hinaufschauen
lucky ['lʌki] glücklich

M

magic ['mædʒɪk] magisch,
  verzaubert
microphone ['maɪkrəfəʊn]
  Mikrofon
mummy ['mʌmi] Mumie
mysterious [mɪ'stɪəriəs]
  geheimnisvoll

N

nail [neɪl] Nagel
nervous ['nɜːvəs] nervös,
  aufgeregt
next [nekst]: **next to** neben

O

object ['ɒbdʒɪkt] Objekt,
  Gegenstand
once [wʌns] einmal
origami [ˌɒrɪ'gɑːmi] Origami
over ['əʊvə]: **over here** hier
  drüben   **over there** dort
  drüben

P

paper clip ['peɪpə_ˌklɪp]
  Büroklammer
(to) park [pɑːk] parken

(to) **pay** [peɪ] bezahlen
pharaoh ['feərəʊ] Pharao
pick [pɪk]: (to) **pick up** sb. jn.
  abholen, mitnehmen
pocket ['pɒkɪt] (Hosen-)Tasche
  pocket money Taschengeld
porcelain ['pɔːsəlɪn] Porzellan
professional [prə'feʃənl]
  professionell
pull [pʊl]: (to) **pull out**
  herausziehen

Q

quickly [kwɪkli] schnell

R

raffle ['ræfl] Verlosung, Tombola
(to) **rain** [reɪn] regnen
rear-view mirror [ˌrɪəvjuː_'mɪrə]
  Rückspiegel
rescue ['reskjuː]: **rescue centre**
  Rettungsstation
(to) **ring** [rɪŋ], **rang** klingeln
ruby ['ruːbi] Rubin
(to) **run off** [ˌrʌn_'ɒf] wegrennen,
  weglaufen

S

(to) **sail** [seɪl] segeln
scared [skeəd] ängstlich
(to) **scratch** [skrætʃ] (sich)
  kratzen
scream [skriːm] Schrei
second-hand [ˌsekənd'hænd]
  gebraucht, aus zweiter Hand
secret ['siːkrət] Geheimnis,
  Geheim-
shock [ʃɒk] Schock, Schreck

shopping centre ['ʃɒpɪŋˌsentə] Einkaufszentrum

should [ʃʊd] sollen

(to) **spend** [spend], **spent** (Geld) ausgeben

stage [steɪdʒ] Bühne

stairs [steəs] Treppe

(to) **stand** [stænd], **stood** stehen   (to) **stand up** aufstehen

statue ['stætʃuː] Statue

strip [strɪp] Streifen

(to) **shuffle sth.** ['ʃʌfl] etwas hin- und herschieben

sidewalk ['saɪdwɔːk] *(AE)* Bürgersteig

(to) **sigh** [saɪ] seufzen

silk [sɪlk] Seide

stuff [stʌf] Dinge, Zeug

such [sʌtʃ] solch

supermarket ['suːpəmɑːkɪt] Supermarkt

sure [ʃʊə]: (to) **be sure** (of sth.) sicher sein, sich etwas sicher sein

T

tail [teɪl] Schwanz

(to) **take off** [ˌteɪkˈɒf] abnehmen (Hut)

tea caddy ['tiːˌkædi] Teedose

terrible ['terəbl] schrecklich

text [tekst] hier: SMS

(to) **thank sb.** [θæŋk] jm. danken

toast [təʊst] Toast

tobacco [təˈbækəʊ] Tabak

tomorrow [təˈmɒrəʊ] morgen

trap [træp] Falle

trumpet ['trʌmpɪt] Trompete

U

ugly ['ʌgli] hässlich

V

valuable ['væljuəbl] wertvoll

vampire ['væmpaɪə] Vampir

W

(to) **walk off** [ˌwɔːkˈɒf] weggehen, verlassen

(to) **wave sth.** [weɪv] mit etwas winken, wedeln

(to) **whisper** ['wɪspə] flüstern

will ('ll) [wɪl] werden **won't** nicht werden

(to) **wonder** ['wʌndə] sich fragen

wood [wʊd]: **piece of wood** Holzstück

world [wɜːld] Welt

(to) **worry** ['wʌri] sich sorgen, beunruhigen

After you read a chapter, try to answer the questions about it. If you know the answers, then go to the next chapter. If you don't know the answers, you can look at the chapter again.

Chapter 1

1 Who meets at Drake Circus Shopping Centre?

2 Why do they meet?

Chapter 2

1 What do Maya and Abby do at the jumble sale?

2 Who did the boys almost hit? What does she look like?

Chapter 3

1 Why does Lucy not talk to Maya?

2 What tickets do Justin, Sam and Lucy buy?

Chapter 4

1 What does Justin win?

Chapter 5

1 What does Justin do with his prize?

2 Who wants Justin's prize? And what does she want to give him for it?

Chapter 6

1 What car is behind Justin's mum?
2 Where do the kids want to go? And when?

Chapter 7

1 Who is also in the Museum?

Chapter 8

1 What do Justin and Sam find out about the box?
2 Who is the girl in the red shirt? What is she doing?
3 What do the boys find in the box?
4 In Poppy's room there's a photo of a woman with the brooch. Who is she?

Chapter 9

1 Who do the boys meet at Poppy's house? Who is she?
2 What is the matter with Poppy?

Chapter 10

1 What does Poppy give Justin as a present?
2 What is the bad news from the USA?